The People's Place Address Book
of Amish Folk Art

Good Books

Intercourse, Pennsylvania 17534

Photos by Jonathan Charles
Design by Craig N. Heisey

The People's Place Address Book of Amish Folk Art
© 1987 by Good Books, Intercourse, Pennsylvania 17534
International Standard Book Number: 0-934672-49-0

A Word about Amish Folk Art

Often seen as an austere group, the Amish have been creators of startlingly beautiful quilts, furniture, bookplates, dolls, and other small handcrafts.

It is the bold and dramatic use of color that makes Amish quilts so memorable. Unencumbered by the convention of "proper" color combinations, Amish women pieced pinks and reds, purples and greens, and reds and blues side by side. The results were striking, especially when done in patterns that had strength because of their simplicity.

The quilting, lavish by contrast to the relatively plain piecing design, is testimony to the love and care that usually surrounded the creation of a quilt. For much Amish folk art was made for family members and, consequently, was an expression of appreciation.

One can also read the values of this religious community in other traditional handcrafts that remain. Samplers and bookplates speak of their respect for extended family and history. In their dolls, stuffed animals, knitted gloves, and socks is delight for children. The furniture, clean and sturdy in its lines and craftsmanship, has warm accents in its detail.

About The People's Place

The People's Place is an Amish-Mennonite heritage center in the quaint village of Intercourse, Pennsylvania, located in the heart of the old Amish settlement. Some of the treasures pictured in this book are on public exhibit at The People's Place.

This educational complex seeks to foster better understanding about our various peoples, our history, lifestyle, faith, and artistic expression.

You may visit our art gallery, pottery gallery, Old Country Store and Old Road Furniture Company also. These shops specialize in handmade creations by local Amish and Mennonite craftspersons and artists.

About the Quilt Museum

The People's Place Quilt Museum is the first permanent museum of antique Amish quilts, one of the rarest and most popular forms of folk art in North America.

Gathered from many Amish communities across the continent, the quilts are displayed in their colorful glory, along with exquisite dolls, toys and socks.

Our staff welcomes you!

-Merle and Phyllis Good
Executive Directors

Sunshine and Shadow Quilt
c. 1920
Lancaster Co., PA
wool
83″ × 83″

Name _____ Phone _____

Address _____ _____

_____ Birthday _____

Name _____ Phone _____

Address _____ _____

_____ Birthday _____

Name _____ Phone _____

Address _____ _____

_____ Birthday _____

Name _____ Phone _____

Address _____ _____

_____ Birthday _____

Name _____ Phone _____

Address _____ _____

_____ Birthday _____

Name _____ Phone _____

Address _____ _____

_____ Birthday _____

Name _____ Phone _____

Address _____ _____

_____ Birthday _____

Name _____ Phone _____

Address _____ _____

_____ Birthday _____

Name _____ Phone _____

Address _____ _____

_____ Birthday _____

Name _____ Phone _____

Address _____ _____

_____ Birthday _____

Name _____ Phone _____

Address _____ _____

_____ Birthday _____

Name _____ Phone _____

Address _____ _____

_____ Birthday _____

Name _____ Phone _____

Address _____ _____

_____ Birthday _____

Name _____ Phone _____

Address _____ _____

_____ Birthday _____

Socks
c. 1900
Lancaster Co., PA
wool

Name _____ Phone _____
Address _____ _____
_____ Birthday _____

Name _____ Phone _____
Address _____ _____
_____ Birthday _____

Name _____ Phone _____
Address _____ _____
_____ Birthday _____

Name _____ Phone _____
Address _____ _____
_____ Birthday _____

Name _____ Phone _____
Address _____ _____
_____ Birthday _____

Name _____ Phone _____
Address _____ _____
_____ Birthday _____

Name _____ Phone _____
Address _____ _____
_____ Birthday _____

Name _____ Phone _____
Address _____ _____
_____ Birthday _____

Name _____ Phone _____
Address _____
         _____ Birthday _____

Name _____ Phone _____
Address _____
         _____ Birthday _____

Name _____ Phone _____
Address _____
         _____ Birthday _____

Name _____ Phone _____
Address _____
         _____ Birthday _____

Name _____ Phone _____
Address _____
         _____ Birthday _____

Name _____ Phone _____
Address _____
         _____ Birthday _____

Name _____ Phone _____
Address _____
         _____ Birthday _____

Name _____ Phone _____
Address _____
         _____ Birthday _____

Name

Address

Phone

Birthday

Name

Address

Phone

Birthday

Name

Address

Phone

Birthday

Name

Address

Phone

Birthday

Name

Address

Phone

Birthday

Name

Address

Phone

Birthday

Name

Address

Phone

Birthday

Name

Address

Phone

Birthday

Name	Phone _____
Address	
	Birthday _____
Name	Phone _____
Address	
	Birthday _____
Name	Phone _____
Address	
	Birthday _____
Name	Phone _____
Address	
	Birthday _____
Name	Phone _____
Address	
	Birthday _____
Name	Phone _____
Address	
	Birthday _____
Name	Phone _____
Address	
	Birthday _____
Name	Phone _____
Address	
	Birthday _____

Name _____ Phone _____

Address _____

_____ Birthday _____

Name _____ Phone _____

Address _____

_____ Birthday _____

Name _____ Phone _____

Address _____

_____ Birthday _____

Name _____ Phone _____

Address _____

_____ Birthday _____

Name _____ Phone _____

Address _____

_____ Birthday _____

Name _____ Phone _____

Address _____

_____ Birthday _____

Name _____ Phone _____

Address _____

_____ Birthday _____

Name _____ Phone _____

Address _____

_____ Birthday _____

Name _____   Phone _____

Address _____   _____

_____   Birthday _____

Name _____   Phone _____

Address _____   _____

_____   Birthday _____

Name _____   Phone _____

Address _____   _____

_____   Birthday _____

Name _____   Phone _____

Address _____   _____

_____   Birthday _____

Name _____   Phone _____

Address _____   _____

_____   Birthday _____

Name _____   Phone _____

Address _____   _____

_____   Birthday _____

Log Cabin Quilt
c. 1930
Medford, WI
cotton
73" × 83"

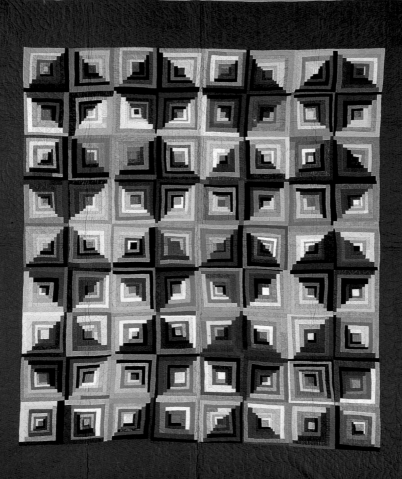

DAVE REINHARD 4MI. NORTH WEST of BERNE
1947 —

Name _____ Phone _____

Address _____

_____ Birthday _____

Name _____ Phone _____

Address _____

_____ Birthday _____

Name _____ Phone _____

Address _____

_____ Birthday _____

Name _____ Phone _____

Address _____

_____ Birthday _____

Name _____ Phone _____

Address _____

_____ Birthday _____

Name _____ Phone _____

Address _____

_____ Birthday _____

Name _____ Phone _____

Address _____

_____ Birthday _____

Name _____ Phone _____

Address _____

_____ Birthday _____

Name _____ Phone _____

Address _____ _____

_____ Birthday _____

Name _____ Phone _____

Address _____ _____

_____ Birthday _____

Name _____ Phone _____

Address _____ _____

_____ Birthday _____

Name _____ Phone _____

Address _____ _____

_____ Birthday _____

Name _____ Phone _____

Address _____ _____

_____ Birthday _____

Name _____ Phone _____

Address _____ _____

_____ Birthday _____

Name _____ Phone _____

Address _____ _____

_____ Birthday _____

Name _____ Phone _____

Address _____ _____

_____ Birthday _____

Name _____ Phone _____

Address _____ _____

_____ Birthday _____

Name _____ Phone _____

Address _____ _____

_____ Birthday _____

Name _____ Phone _____

Address _____ _____

_____ Birthday _____

Name _____ Phone _____

Address _____ _____

_____ Birthday _____

Name _____ Phone _____

Address _____ _____

_____ Birthday _____

Name _____ Phone _____

Address _____ _____

_____ Birthday _____

Name _____ Phone _____

Address _____ _____

_____ Birthday _____

Name _____ Phone _____

Address _____ _____

_____ Birthday _____

Name _____ Phone _____
Address _____
_____ Birthday _____

Name _____ Phone _____
Address _____
_____ Birthday _____

Name _____ Phone _____
Address _____
_____ Birthday _____

Name _____ Phone _____
Address _____
_____ Birthday _____

Name _____ Phone _____
Address _____
_____ Birthday _____

Name _____ Phone _____
Address _____
_____ Birthday _____

Name _____ Phone _____
Address _____
_____ Birthday _____

Name _____ Phone _____
Address _____
_____ Birthday _____

Name

Address

Phone

Birthday

Name

Address

Phone

Birthday

Name

Address

Phone

Birthday

Name

Address

Phone

Birthday

Name

Address

Phone

Birthday

Name

Address

Phone

Birthday

Name

Address

Phone

Birthday

Name

Address

Phone

Birthday

Name _____ Phone _____

Address _____ _____

_____ Birthday _____

Name _____ Phone _____

Address _____ _____

_____ Birthday _____

Name _____ Phone _____

Address _____ _____

_____ Birthday _____

Name _____ Phone _____

Address _____ _____

_____ Birthday _____

Name _____ Phone _____

Address _____ _____

_____ Birthday _____

Name _____ Phone _____

Address _____ _____

_____ Birthday _____

Dutch Cupboard
c. 1890
Lancaster Co., PA
Made by Henry Lapp
walnut
$76^{1}/_{2}'' \times 53'' \times 19^{3}/_{4}''$

Name

Address

Phone

Birthday

Name

Address

Phone

Birthday

Name

Address

Phone

Birthday

Name

Address

Phone

Birthday

Name

Address

Phone

Birthday

Name

Address

Phone

Birthday

Name

Address

Phone

Birthday

Name

Address

Phone

Birthday

Name

Address

_____

Phone _____

_____

Birthday _____

Name

Address

_____

Phone _____

_____

Birthday _____

Name

Address

_____

Phone _____

_____

Birthday _____

Name

Address

_____

Phone _____

_____

Birthday _____

Name

Address

_____

Phone _____

_____

Birthday _____

Name

Address

_____

Phone _____

_____

Birthday _____

Name

Address

_____

Phone _____

_____

Birthday _____

Name

Address

_____

Phone _____

_____

Birthday _____

Name	Phone
Address	
	Birthday

Name	Phone
Address	
	Birthday

Name	Phone
Address	
	Birthday

Name	Phone
Address	
	Birthday

Name	Phone
Address	
	Birthday

Name	Phone
Address	
	Birthday

Name	Phone
Address	
	Birthday

Name	Phone
Address	
	Birthday

Name _____   Phone _____

Address _____

_____   Birthday _____

Name _____   Phone _____

Address _____

_____   Birthday _____

Name _____   Phone _____

Address _____

_____   Birthday _____

Name _____   Phone _____

Address _____

_____   Birthday _____

Name _____   Phone _____

Address _____

_____   Birthday _____

Name _____   Phone _____

Address _____

_____   Birthday _____

Indiana Puzzle Quilt
c. late 1930s
Holmes Co., OH
cotton
68″ × 82″

Name

Address

Phone

Birthday

Name

Address

Phone

Birthday

Name

Address

Phone

Birthday

Name

Address

Phone

Birthday

Name

Address

Phone

Birthday

Name

Address

Phone

Birthday

Name

Address

Phone

Birthday

Name

Address

Phone

Birthday

Name _____ Phone _____

Address _____

_____ Birthday _____

Name _____ Phone _____

Address _____

_____ Birthday _____

Name _____ Phone _____

Address _____

_____ Birthday _____

Name _____ Phone _____

Address _____

_____ Birthday _____

Name _____ Phone _____

Address _____

_____ Birthday _____

Name _____ Phone _____

Address _____

_____ Birthday _____

Name _____ Phone _____

Address _____

_____ Birthday _____

Name _____ Phone _____

Address _____

_____ Birthday _____

Name

Address

Phone

Birthday

Name

Address

Phone

Birthday

Name

Address

Phone

Birthday

Name

Address

Phone

Birthday

Name

Address

Phone

Birthday

Name

Address

Phone

Birthday

Name

Address

Phone

Birthday

Name

Address

Phone

Birthday

Name _____ Phone _____

Address _____

_____ Birthday _____

Name _____ Phone _____

Address _____

_____ Birthday _____

Name _____ Phone _____

Address _____

_____ Birthday _____

Name _____ Phone _____

Address _____

_____ Birthday _____

Name _____ Phone _____

Address _____

_____ Birthday _____

Name _____ Phone _____

Address _____

_____ Birthday _____

Stuffed Horse
c. 1910
$7'' \times 7^{1}/_{2}''$

Name

Address

Phone _____

Birthday _____

Name

Address

Phone _____

Birthday _____

Name

Address

Phone _____

Birthday _____

Name

Address

Phone _____

Birthday _____

Name

Address

Phone _____

Birthday _____

Name

Address

Phone _____

Birthday _____

Name

Address

Phone _____

Birthday _____

Name

Address

Phone _____

Birthday _____

Name

Address

Phone

Birthday

Name

Address

Phone

Birthday

Name

Address

Phone

Birthday

Name

Address

Phone

Birthday

Name

Address

Phone

Birthday

Name

Address

Phone

Birthday

Double Wedding Ring Quilt
c. 1940
Holmes Co., OH
cotton
77" × 93"

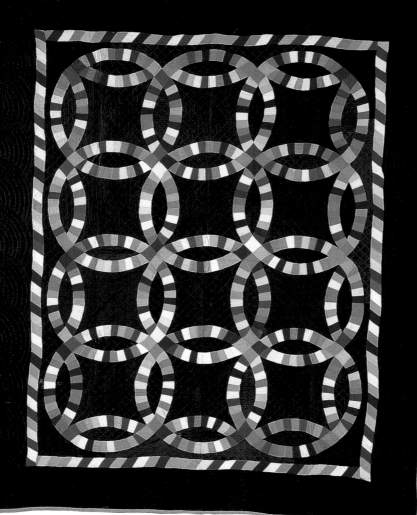

Lidia Schmucker
Gehöret Dießes
Büchlein zu

Geschriben Den
28 ten September
1 8   7 1

Barbara Eberßol

Name

Address

Phone _____

Birthday _____

Name

Address

Phone _____

Birthday _____

Name

Address

Phone _____

Birthday _____

Name

Address

Phone _____

Birthday _____

Name

Address

Phone _____

Birthday _____

Name

Address

Phone _____

Birthday _____

Name

Address

Phone _____

Birthday _____

Name

Address

Phone _____

Birthday _____

Name _____ Phone _____

Address _____ _____

_____ Birthday _____

Name _____ Phone _____

Address _____ _____

_____ Birthday _____

Name _____ Phone _____

Address _____ _____

_____ Birthday _____

Name _____ Phone _____

Address _____ _____

_____ Birthday _____

Name _____ Phone _____

Address _____ _____

_____ Birthday _____

Name _____ Phone _____

Address _____ _____

_____ Birthday _____

Name _____ Phone _____

Address _____ _____

_____ Birthday _____

Name _____ Phone _____

Address _____ _____

_____ Birthday _____

Name

Address

Phone _____

Birthday _____

Name

Address

Phone _____

Birthday _____

Name

Address

Phone _____

Birthday _____

Name

Address

Phone _____

Birthday _____

Name

Address

Phone _____

Birthday _____

Name

Address

Phone _____

Birthday _____

Name

Address

Phone _____

Birthday _____

Name

Address

Phone _____

Birthday _____

Name _____ Phone _____

Address _____ _____

_____ Birthday _____

Name _____ Phone _____

Address _____ _____

_____ Birthday _____

Name _____ Phone _____

Address _____ _____

_____ Birthday _____

Name _____ Phone _____

Address _____ _____

_____ Birthday _____

Name _____ Phone _____

Address _____ _____

_____ Birthday _____

Name _____ Phone _____

Address _____ _____

_____ Birthday _____

Pincushions
c. 1910–1940
Pennsylvania, Iowa, unknown
cotton, wool
1″–5″

Name

Address

Phone _____

Birthday _____

Name

Address

Phone _____

Birthday _____

Name

Address

Phone _____

Birthday _____

Name

Address

Phone _____

Birthday _____

Name

Address

Phone _____

Birthday _____

Name

Address

Phone _____

Birthday _____

Name

Address

Phone _____

Birthday _____

Name

Address

Phone _____

Birthday _____

Name

Address

Phone _____

Birthday _____

Name

Address

Phone _____

Birthday _____

Name

Address

Phone _____

Birthday _____

Name

Address

Phone _____

Birthday _____

Name

Address

Phone _____

Birthday _____

Name

Address

Phone _____

Birthday _____

Railroad Crossing Quilt
1942
Holmes Co., OH
cotton
68″ × 85″

Name

Address

Phone _____

Birthday _____

Name

Address

Phone _____

Birthday _____

Name

Address

Phone _____

Birthday _____

Name

Address

Phone _____

Birthday _____

Name

Address

Phone _____

Birthday _____

Name

Address

Phone _____

Birthday _____

Mittens/Gloves
c. 1900–1940
Lancaster Co. and Somerset Co., PA
wool

Name _____ Phone _____

Address _____

_____ Birthday _____

Name _____ Phone _____

Address _____

_____ Birthday _____

Name _____ Phone _____

Address _____

_____ Birthday _____

Name _____ Phone _____

Address _____

_____ Birthday _____

Name _____ Phone _____

Address _____

_____ Birthday _____

Name _____ Phone _____

Address _____

_____ Birthday _____

Name _____ Phone _____

Address _____

_____ Birthday _____

Name _____ Phone _____

Address _____

_____ Birthday _____

Name

Address

Phone _____

Birthday _____

Name

Address

Phone _____

Birthday _____

Name

Address

Phone _____

Birthday _____

Name

Address

Phone _____

Birthday _____

Name

Address

Phone _____

Birthday _____

Name

Address

Phone _____

Birthday _____

Name

Address

Phone _____

Birthday _____

Name

Address

Phone _____

Birthday _____

Name _____ Phone _____
Address _____ _____
_____ Birthday _____

Name _____ Phone _____
Address _____ _____
_____ Birthday _____

Name _____ Phone _____
Address _____ _____
_____ Birthday _____

Name _____ Phone _____
Address _____ _____
_____ Birthday _____

Name _____ Phone _____
Address _____ _____
_____ Birthday _____

Name _____ Phone _____
Address _____ _____
_____ Birthday _____

Name _____ Phone _____
Address _____ _____
_____ Birthday _____

Name _____ Phone _____
Address _____ _____
_____ Birthday _____

Name

Address

Phone _____

Birthday _____

Name

Address

Phone _____

Birthday _____

Name

Address

Phone _____

Birthday _____

Name

Address

Phone _____

Birthday _____

Name

Address

Phone _____

Birthday _____

Name

Address

Phone _____

Birthday _____

Name

Address

Phone _____

Birthday _____

Name

Address

Phone _____

Birthday _____

Name _____ Phone _____
Address _____ _____
_____ Birthday _____

Name _____ Phone _____
Address _____ _____
_____ Birthday _____

Name _____ Phone _____
Address _____ _____
_____ Birthday _____

Name _____ Phone _____
Address _____ _____
_____ Birthday _____

Name _____ Phone _____
Address _____ _____
_____ Birthday _____

Name _____ Phone _____
Address _____ _____
_____ Birthday _____

Doll
c. 1940
Ohio
15" high

Name _Lenore_ 651-201-7062 Phone _____

Address _____

_____ Birthday _____

Name _N. Lindberg_ Phone _____

Address _69 e grden lake Rd_ _C Pines_

_763 780 6377_ Birthday _____

Name _L. Clair_ Phone _____

Address _763 263 1140_

_" 482 0170_ Birthday _____

Name _____ Phone _____

Address _____

_____ Birthday _____

Name _____ Phone _____

Address _____

_____ Birthday _____

Name _____ Phone _____

Address _____

_____ Birthday _____

Baskets Quilt
c. 1930
New Wilmington, PA
cotton
$73\frac{1}{2}$" × $82\frac{1}{2}$"

Name	Phone _____
Address	
_____	Birthday _____
Name	Phone _____
Address	
_____	Birthday _____
Name	Phone _____
Address	
_____	Birthday _____
Name	Phone _____
Address	
_____	Birthday _____
Name	Phone _____
Address	
_____	Birthday _____
Name	Phone _____
Address	
_____	Birthday _____
Name	Phone _____
Address	
_____	Birthday _____
Name	Phone _____
Address	
_____	Birthday _____

Name	Phone _____
Address	
_____	Birthday _____
Name	Phone _____
Address	
_____	Birthday _____
Name	Phone _____
Address	
_____	Birthday _____
Name	Phone _____
Address	
_____	Birthday _____
Name	Phone _____
Address	
_____	Birthday _____
Name	Phone _____
Address	
_____	Birthday _____
Name	Phone _____
Address	
_____	Birthday _____
Name	Phone _____
Address	
_____	Birthday _____

Name _____ Phone _____

Address _____

_____ Birthday _____

Name _____ Phone _____

Address _____

_____ Birthday _____

Name _____ Phone _____

Address _____

_____ Birthday _____

Name _____ Phone _____

Address _____

_____ Birthday _____

Name _____ Phone _____

Address _____

_____ Birthday _____

Name _____ Phone _____

Address _____

_____ Birthday _____

Name _____ Phone _____

Address _____

_____ Birthday _____

Name _____ Phone _____

Address _____

_____ Birthday _____

Name _____ Phone _____
Address _____
_____ _____
_____ Birthday _____

Name _____ Phone _____
Address _____
_____ _____
_____ Birthday _____

Name _____ Phone _____
Address _____
_____ _____
_____ Birthday _____

Name _____ Phone _____
Address _____
_____ _____
_____ Birthday _____

Name _____ Phone _____
Address _____
_____ _____
_____ Birthday _____

Name _____ Phone _____
Address _____
_____ _____
_____ Birthday _____

Name _____ Phone _____
Address _____
_____ _____
_____ Birthday _____

Name _____ Phone _____
Address _____
_____ _____
_____ Birthday _____

Name _____   Phone _____

Address _____

_____   Birthday _____

Name _____   Phone _____

Address _____

_____   Birthday _____

Name _____   Phone _____

Address _____

_____   Birthday _____

Name _____   Phone _____

Address _____

_____   Birthday _____

Name _____   Phone _____

Address _____

_____   Birthday _____

Name _____   Phone _____

Address _____

_____   Birthday _____

Carolina Lily Quilt
c. 1920–30
Holmes Co., OH
cotton
67″ × 86″

Name	Melon 598 4919	Phone _____
Address	925 - 3459	_____
		Birthday _____
Name	Joanne 242 8822	Phone _____
Address	729 8723	
	4719 30th	Birthday _____
Name	Mazur	Phone _____
Address	319 277 7449	
	504 3553	Birthday _____
Name	Joel 701- 772 1108	Phone _____
Address		
		Birthday _____
Name	Jared 636 1261	Phone _____
Address	1917 Enfal	
	55403	Birthday _____
Name	John	Phone _____
Address	218 255 1381	
	218 652 3602	Birthday _____

Bentwood Hickory Rocker
c. 1930
Ohio
42″ × 33″

Name _____ Phone _____

Address _____ _____

_____ Birthday _____

Name _____ Phone _____

Address _____ _____

_____ Birthday _____

Name _____ Phone _____

Address _____ _____

_____ Birthday _____

Name _____ Phone _____

Address _____ _____

_____ Birthday _____

Name _____ Phone _____

Address _____ _____

_____ Birthday _____

Name _____ Phone _____

Address _____ _____

_____ Birthday _____

Name _____ Phone _____

Address _____ _____

_____ Birthday _____

Name _____ Phone _____

Address _____ _____

_____ Birthday _____

Name	Marie Mayher	Phone _____
Address	651 649 1505	_____
		Birthday _____
Name	Judy McDougal	Phone _____
Address		
	952 426 5581	Birthday _____
Name		Phone _____
Address		
		Birthday _____
Name		Phone _____
Address		
		Birthday _____
Name		Phone _____
Address		
		Birthday _____
Name		Phone _____
Address		
		Birthday _____
Name		Phone _____
Address		
		Birthday _____
Name		Phone _____
Address		
		Birthday _____

Name Susan M.

Address 541 - 410 - 3636

Phone _____

_____

Birthday _____

Name Mazur

Address

1-319 2777449

Phone _____

_____

Birthday _____

Name Jay

Address

Phone _____

_____

Birthday _____

Name Muster

Address 4725 D.

8229660

Phone _____

_____

Birthday _____

Name

Address

Phone _____

_____

Birthday _____

Name

Address

Phone _____

_____

Birthday _____

Name

Address

Phone _____

_____

Birthday _____

Name

Address

Phone _____

_____

Birthday _____

Name

Address

Phone _____

Birthday _____

Name

Address

Phone _____

Birthday _____

Name

Address

Phone _____

Birthday _____

Name

Address

Phone _____

Birthday _____

Name

Address

Phone _____

Birthday _____

Name

Address

Phone _____

Birthday _____

Name

Address

Phone _____

Birthday _____

Name

Address

Phone _____

Birthday _____

Name Marin
Address
412-0851
Phone _____

Birthday _____

Name Missy
Address 208 2nd St SW
218-773 1282
Phone _____

Birthday _____

Name John
Address Nevis 56467
218- 652 3602
Phone _____

Birthday _____

Name Jane
Address 3110 et 23
ashley
218 255 0287
Phone _____

Birthday _____

Name
Address
Phone _____

Birthday _____

Name
Address
Phone _____

Birthday _____

Name
Address
Phone _____

Birthday _____

Name
Address
Phone _____

Birthday _____

Name

Address

Phone _____

Birthday _____

Name

Address

Phone _____

Birthday _____

Name

Address

Phone _____

Birthday _____

Name

Address

Phone _____

Birthday _____

Name

Address

Phone _____

Birthday _____

Name

Address

Phone _____

Birthday _____

Name

Address

Phone _____

Birthday _____

Name

Address

Phone _____

Birthday _____

Name _____ Phone _____

Address _____ _____

_____ Birthday _____

Name _____ Phone _____

Address _____ _____

_____ Birthday _____

Name _____ Phone _____

Address _____ _____

_____ Birthday _____

Name _____ Phone _____

Address _____ _____

_____ Birthday _____

Name _____ Phone _____

Address _____ _____

_____ Birthday _____

Name _____ Phone _____

Address _____ _____

_____ Birthday _____

Show Towel
1902
Mifflin Co., PA
linen
$40^{1}/_{2}'' \times 17''$

N

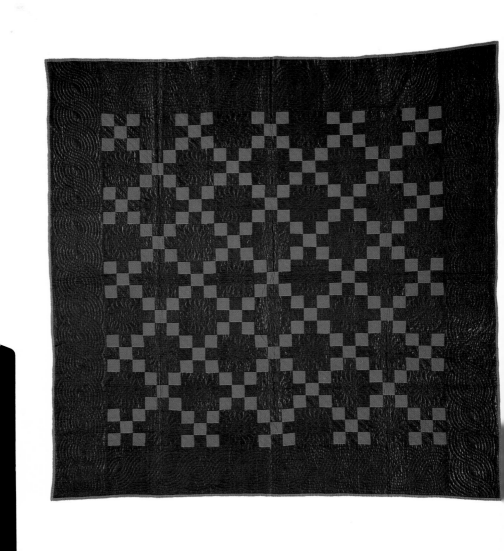

Name _____ Phone _____

Address _____

_____ Birthday _____

Name _____ Phone _____

Address _____

_____ Birthday _____

Name _____ Phone _____

Address _____

_____ Birthday _____

Name _____ Phone _____

Address _____

_____ Birthday _____

Name _____ Phone _____

Address _____

_____ Birthday _____

Name _____ Phone _____

Address _____

_____ Birthday _____

Single Irish Chain Quilt
c. 1890s
Holmes Co., OH
cotton
84″ × 86″

Name _____ Phone _____
Address _____
_____ Birthday _____

Name _____ Phone _____
Address _____
_____ Birthday _____

Name _____ Phone _____
Address _____
_____ Birthday _____

Name _____ Phone _____
Address _____
_____ Birthday _____

Name _____ Phone _____
Address _____
_____ Birthday _____

Name _____ Phone _____
Address _____
_____ Birthday _____

Name _____ Phone _____
Address _____
_____ Birthday _____

Name _____ Phone _____
Address _____
_____ Birthday _____

Name

Address

Phone _____

Birthday _____

Name

Address

Phone _____

Birthday _____

Name

Address

Phone _____

Birthday _____

Name

Address

Phone _____

Birthday _____

Name

Address

Phone _____

Birthday _____

Name

Address

Phone _____

Birthday _____

Name

Address

Phone _____

Birthday _____

Name

Address

Phone _____

Birthday _____

Name _____ Phone _____

Address _____ _____

_____ Birthday _____

Name _____ Phone _____

Address _____ _____

_____ Birthday _____

Name _____ Phone _____

Address _____ _____

_____ Birthday _____

Name _____ Phone _____

Address _____ _____

_____ Birthday _____

Name _____ Phone _____

Address _____ _____

_____ Birthday _____

Name _____ Phone _____

Address _____ _____

_____ Birthday _____

Crazy Quilt
c. 1940
Lancaster Co., PA
crepe, cotton, wool
82″ × 82″

PQ

Name

Address

Phone

Birthday

Name

Address

Phone

Birthday

Name

Address

Phone

Birthday

Name

Address

Phone

Birthday

Name

Address

Phone

Birthday

Name

Address

Phone

Birthday

Name

Address

Phone

Birthday

Name

Address

Phone

Birthday

Name _____ Phone _____

Address _____

_____ Birthday _____

Name _____ Phone _____

Address _____

_____ Birthday _____

Name _____ Phone _____

Address _____

_____ Birthday _____

Name _____ Phone _____

Address _____

_____ Birthday _____

Name _____ Phone _____

Address _____

_____ Birthday _____

Name _____ Phone _____

Address _____

_____ Birthday _____

Name _____ Phone _____

Address _____

_____ Birthday _____

Name _____ Phone _____

Address _____

_____ Birthday _____

Name _____ Phone _____

Address _____

_____ Birthday _____

Name _____ Phone _____

Address _____

_____ Birthday _____

Name _____ Phone _____

Address _____

_____ Birthday _____

Name _____ Phone _____

Address _____

_____ Birthday _____

Name _____ Phone _____

Address _____

_____ Birthday _____

Name _____ Phone _____

Address _____

_____ Birthday _____

Name _____ Phone _____

Address _____

_____ Birthday _____

Name _____ Phone _____

Address _____

_____ Birthday _____

Name _____ Phone _____

Address _____ _____

_____ Birthday _____

Name _____ Phone _____

Address _____ _____

_____ Birthday _____

Name _____ Phone _____

Address _____ _____

_____ Birthday _____

Name _____ Phone _____

Address _____ _____

_____ Birthday _____

Name _____ Phone _____

Address _____ _____

_____ Birthday _____

Name _____ Phone _____

Address _____ _____

_____ Birthday _____

Crown of Thorns Quilt
c. 1930
Holmes Co., OH
cotton
80″ × 82″

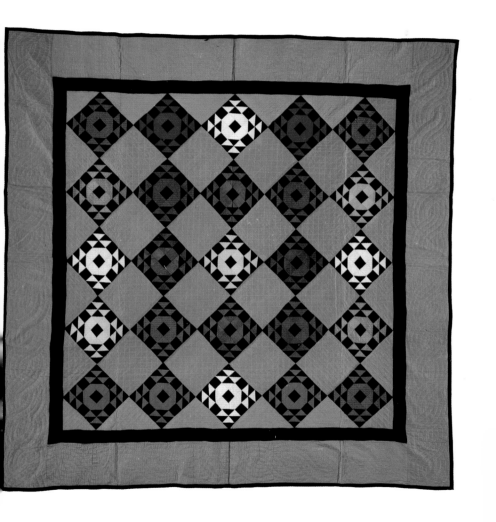

R

Name

Address

Phone

Birthday

Name

Address

Phone

Birthday

Name

Address

Phone

Birthday

Name

Address

Phone

Birthday

Name

Address

Phone

Birthday

Name

Address

Phone

Birthday

Name

Address

Phone

Birthday

Name

Address

Phone

Birthday

Name _____ Phone _____
Address _____ _____
_____ Birthday _____

Name _____ Phone _____
Address _____ _____
_____ Birthday _____

Name _____ Phone _____
Address _____ _____
_____ Birthday _____

Name _____ Phone _____
Address _____ _____
_____ Birthday _____

Name _____ Phone _____
Address _____ _____
_____ Birthday _____

Name _____ Phone _____
Address _____ _____
_____ Birthday _____

Name _____ Phone _____
Address _____ _____
_____ Birthday _____

Name _____ Phone _____
Address _____ _____
_____ Birthday _____

Name

Address

Phone

Birthday

Name

Address

Phone

Birthday

Name

Address

Phone

Birthday

Name

Address

Phone

Birthday

Name

Address

Phone

Birthday

Name

Address

Phone

Birthday

Name

Address

Phone

Birthday

Name

Address

Phone

Birthday

Name _____   Phone _____
Address _____   _____
_____   Birthday _____

Name _____   Phone _____
Address _____   _____
_____   Birthday _____

Name _____   Phone _____
Address _____   _____
_____   Birthday _____

Name _____   Phone _____
Address _____   _____
_____   Birthday _____

Name _____   Phone _____
Address _____   _____
_____   Birthday _____

Name _____   Phone _____
Address _____   _____
_____   Birthday _____

Blanket Chest
1887
Lancaster Co., PA
Made by Henry Lapp
poplar
50″ × 29″ × 24″

S

Name _Sally_ _____ Phone _____

Address _____

_____ Birthday _____

Name _____ Phone _____

Address _____

_____ Birthday _____

Name _____ Phone _____

Address _____

_____ Birthday _____

Name _____ Phone _____

Address _____

_____ Birthday _____

Name _____ Phone _____

Address _____

_____ Birthday _____

Name _____ Phone _____

Address _____

_____ Birthday _____

Name _____ Phone _____

Address _____

_____ Birthday _____

Name _____ Phone _____

Address _____

_____ Birthday _____

Name _____ Phone _____

Address _____ _____

_____ Birthday _____

Name _____ Phone _____

Address _____ _____

_____ Birthday _____

Name _____ Phone _____

Address _____ _____

_____ Birthday _____

Name _____ Phone _____

Address _____ _____

_____ Birthday _____

Name _____ Phone _____

Address _____ _____

_____ Birthday _____

Name _____ Phone _____

Address _____ _____

_____ Birthday _____

Name _____ Phone _____

Address _____ _____

_____ Birthday _____

Name _____ Phone _____

Address _____ _____

_____ Birthday _____

Name _____ Phone _____

Address _____

_____ Birthday _____

Name _____ Phone _____

Address _____

_____ Birthday _____

Name _____ Phone _____

Address _____

_____ Birthday _____

Name _____ Phone _____

Address _____

_____ Birthday _____

Name _____ Phone _____

Address _____

_____ Birthday _____

Name _____ Phone _____

Address _____

_____ Birthday _____

Name _____ Phone _____

Address _____

_____ Birthday _____

Name _____ Phone _____

Address _____

_____ Birthday _____

Name _____   Phone _____

Address _____   _____

_____   Birthday _____

Name _____   Phone _____

Address _____   _____

_____   Birthday _____

Name _____   Phone _____

Address _____   _____

_____   Birthday _____

Name _____   Phone _____

Address _____   _____

_____   Birthday _____

Name _____   Phone _____

Address _____   _____

_____   Birthday _____

Name _____   Phone _____

Address _____   _____

_____   Birthday _____

Dresden Plate
c. 1910
Holmes Co., OH
cotton
80″ × 75

T

Anna
Stoufusz
1 8 64
Barbera
Eberson

UV

Name _____ Phone _____

Address _____

_____ Birthday _____

Name _____ Phone _____

Address _____

_____ Birthday _____

Name _____ Phone _____

Address _____

_____ Birthday _____

Name _____ Phone _____

Address _____

_____ Birthday _____

Name _____ Phone _____

Address _____

_____ Birthday _____

Name _____ Phone _____

Address _____

_____ Birthday _____

Name _____ Phone _____

Address _____

_____ Birthday _____

Name _____ Phone _____

Address _____

_____ Birthday _____

Name	Phone _____
Address	_____
_____	Birthday _____

Name	Phone _____
Address	_____
_____	Birthday _____

Name	Phone _____
Address	_____
_____	Birthday _____

Name	Phone _____
Address	_____
_____	Birthday _____

Name	Phone _____
Address	_____
_____	Birthday _____

Name	Phone _____
Address	_____
_____	Birthday _____

Triple Irish Chain Quilt
c. 1930
Lancaster Co., PA
wool
85″ × 85″

WX

Name

Address

Phone

Birthday

Name

Address

Phone

Birthday

Name 2601 *Kinju*

Address

Phone

Birthday

Name

Address

Phone

Birthday

Name

Address

Phone

Birthday

Name

Address

Phone

Birthday

Name

Address

Phone

Birthday

Name

Address

Phone

Birthday

Name _____ Phone _____

Address _____

_____ Birthday _____

Name _____ Phone _____

Address _____

_____ Birthday _____

Name _____ Phone _____

Address _____

_____ Birthday _____

Name _____ Phone _____

Address _____

_____ Birthday _____

Name _____ Phone _____

Address _____

_____ Birthday _____

Name _____ Phone _____

Address _____

_____ Birthday _____

Name _____ Phone _____

Address _____

_____ Birthday _____

Name _____ Phone _____

Address _____

_____ Birthday _____

Name _____   Phone _____
Address _____   _____
_____   Birthday _____

Name _____   Phone _____
Address _____   _____
_____   Birthday _____

Name _____   Phone _____
Address _____   _____
_____   Birthday _____

Name _____   Phone _____
Address _____   _____
_____   Birthday _____

Name _____   Phone _____
Address _____   _____
_____   Birthday _____

Name _____   Phone _____
Address _____   _____
_____   Birthday _____

Name _____   Phone _____
Address _____   _____
_____   Birthday _____

Name _____   Phone _____
Address _____   _____
_____   Birthday _____

Name _____ Phone _____

Address _____ _____

_____ Birthday _____

Name _____ Phone _____

Address _____ _____

_____ Birthday _____

Name _____ Phone _____

Address _____ _____

_____ Birthday _____

Name _____ Phone _____

Address _____ _____

_____ Birthday _____

Name _____ Phone _____

Address _____ _____

_____ Birthday _____

Name _____ Phone _____

Address _____ _____

_____ Birthday _____

Doll
c. 1940
Iowa
10½″ high

YZ